Boatbuilding For Beginners

Everything You Need To Know To Build, Paint And Fiberglass Your Boat

Copyright@2023

Giddy Kent

Table of content

CHAPTER ONE

Instructional Guide To Build A Boat

Trips around the lake in a little boat are the ideal way to spend the day. Since they can be stored on the top of your vehicle or in the rear of your truck bed, they are ideal for impromptu visits to the campground. The stitch and glue technique of boat construction is used throughout the construction of a canoe that is 12 feet long by 30 inches wide and has a depth of 11 inches.

Section 1-Constructing The Frame

1-The first step in constructing the frame is to cut and join the plywood panels.

Cut two sheets that are 4' x 8' and 1/8" thick "(door skin plywood) should be cut into sheets that are 24 inches wide. These sheets should then be stacked and attached to one another at the top and bottom edges using tiny nails in a few areas.

2-Marking out your dimensions/measurements.

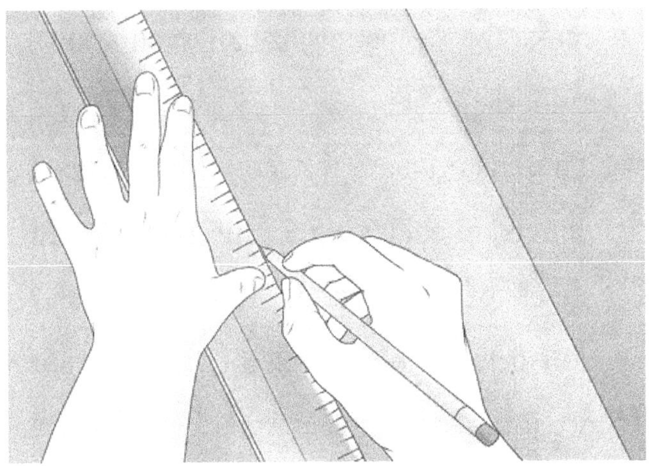

Mark a vertical line at intervals of 12 on the attached panels as you lay them out "through the whole of the plywood's length of 8 feet. In consideration of these 12 "vertical lines, and the marking of points along these lines, you are able to get more accurate measurements..

- It is necessary to use a long stick or batten in order to draw a line between these places in order to create the outlines of the canoe's panels. Check to see that the curves of the lines you make for the panels are all even and smooth.

- There is no need for more than three panels on each side. Using the four half sheets of 8' plywood, 12 boat panels are constructed. Next, these 12 boat panels are joined together in matching pairs using butt blocks or scarf joints to create a total of 6 panels, with three located on each side of the boat.

- Joining the panels together using finger joints, utilizing a dovetail template and a router are additional effective methods of joint construction. You can't forget about the 1, no matter what "overlap of each panel in the process of building the finger joint since doing so

gives the boat an appealing appearance
once it is done.

- This approach may be used to construct
  a boat that is not only easy to use but
  also rather lovely. The resulting vessel
  resembles a canoe in both appearance
  and form and has a shallow "v" rather
  than a flat bottom.

3-Make the cuts in the panels.

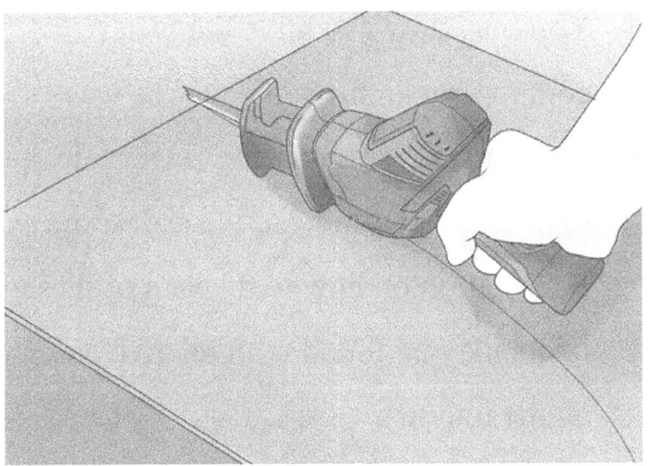

After the panels have been sketched out
and examined to ensure that they have

attractively curved lines, you can now cut them out utilizing a saber saw.

- After you have cut out the panels, use a woodworker's rasp (also known as a file) to smooth down the edges of the panel so that they are as near as possible to the lines that are on the panel. In its place, one may make use of a little block plane.

- You may now assemble the panel components in the same way as was described before by using finger joints, scarves, or butt blocks. More detailed information on how to do each of these joints may be found with relative ease on the internet.

4-**Make holes in the panels by drilling them**.

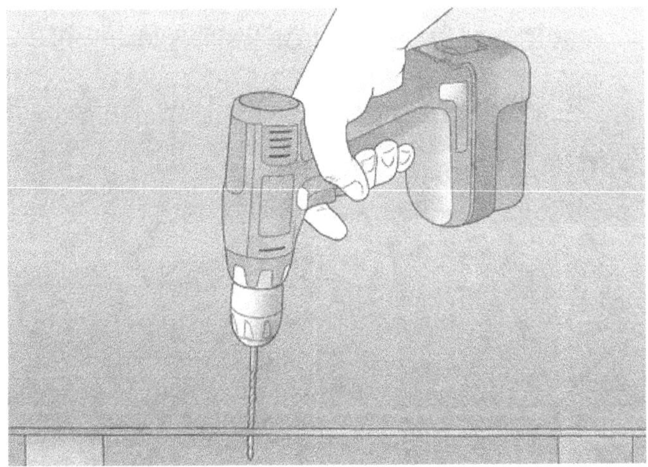

Drill several holes along the bottom edges of the panels, approximately 3/8 of an inch apart, now that the panels have been completed "beginning at the panel's top and bottom edges and working our way up.

- If you arrange the two matching panels (the panels that correspond on each side) together and then drill the holes, this task will be much simpler and will take much less time.

- This canoe only has three panels on each side, and each of those panels is the same on both sides of the canoe.

5-Stitch the panels together.

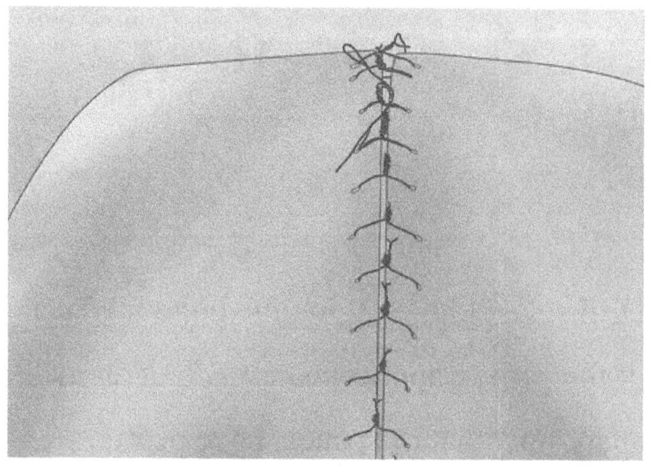

You may get some bailing, copper, or any other kind of wire that is flexible and simple to bend at the hardware shop. Cut the wire into short pieces, about three inches long "long, you will want quite a number of them, around the same amount as would fit in a pie plate. On the other hand, you can always cut more if you find that you need them.

- Placing the two bottom panels on top of each other, then wiring the middle and bottom borders together while being careful not to pull the wire too tightly will complete this step. If you leave the wire slack, the bottom two panels will open up like a book. This part of the canoe will serve as the bottom.

- Now, begin wiring (stitching) on the next panel by placing a few stitches on each side of the center line. Begin at the middle and go outward from there. Continue moving from one side to the next and doing a few actions on each side until you reach the ends.

- When you reach the top panels, you will need to align the ends so that they may be stitched together. Make an effort to make them as equal as you can, and give the canoe ends a lovely bend. At this stage, you should start to watch the boat take shape before your own eyes.

6-Reviewing of your work.

After the panels have been sewn together, position a stick on the inside of the canoe that is about 1 inch square and 29 inches long at the top center. This will ensure that it maintains the correct width and shape.

Now, take a deep breath and carefully analyze the situation.

- Is it straightforward, with excellent flowing lines, and does it not include any twists? If not, adjust the wire stitches so that they are as slack or as tight as the situation calls for, or even add a stitch if required. Check that it has an appealing visual appearance.
- Using winding sticks, you should determine whether or not the canoe has any twists in it. Check that the panel edges are all resting on top of each other in a smooth and tight manner and that there is no overlapping occurring at any time.
- You may also execute a technique that is called cutting a transition joint. This involves cutting a notch that is either 1/4 or 3/8 inches deep into the bottom

front edge of the top panels. The width
of the panel as well as the length of the
canoe are the factors that decide how
deep the notch should be. You will now
have a lovely smooth side as a result.
You may find several books that
address stitch and glue boat
construction on the market nowadays,
as well as more in-depth instructions on
how to perform a transition joint by
searching for them online.

- Last but not least, check that the panels
  are not pulled apart from one other at
  any one location; you want the seams
  to be nice and smooth sewn.

Section 2-Attaching The Panels To The Frame

1-Coat the surface with epoxy.

Create a mixture of epoxy that is just sufficient to fill the seams between the panels. This is accomplished by use a mixing cup with a capacity of 8 ounces and a stick. After that, apply the epoxy to the joints using a foam paint brush.

- If you want a strong connection, you should try to cover each edge about an inch on each side of the joint, and you should make sure that it soaks into the joint. Create the illusion that you are painting a strip along the middle of the joint. Keep in mind that for the time being, the epoxies will only be used on the inside of the panel and stem joints.

- It is necessary to carry out this procedure for each of the joints. You should make every effort to prevent the epoxy from running down the edges of the panels; you only want it on the connection; there should be no runs. If there are any runs, you should use a different brush to clean them up. When it comes to sanding the inside of the boat, this only makes things simpler for the sanding process. Don't forget to inspect the seams on the exterior of the garment as well for any runs.

- Apply two coats of epoxy to the joints
  and stems of the boat, allowing each
  coat of epoxy to cure in between
  applications. The stems are the most
  front parts of the boat. Before you
  begin to apply the epoxy, you need to
  make sure that the stems are stitched
  together and pushed together securely.
  Never use clamps to bring the two ends
  of the stems together; instead, use
  stitches.

- Because each layer of epoxy requires
  around 24 hours to cure, try to exercise
  some patience as you daydream about a
  lake that is perfectly smooth and
  crystalline.

2-Take out the wire stitches in the work.

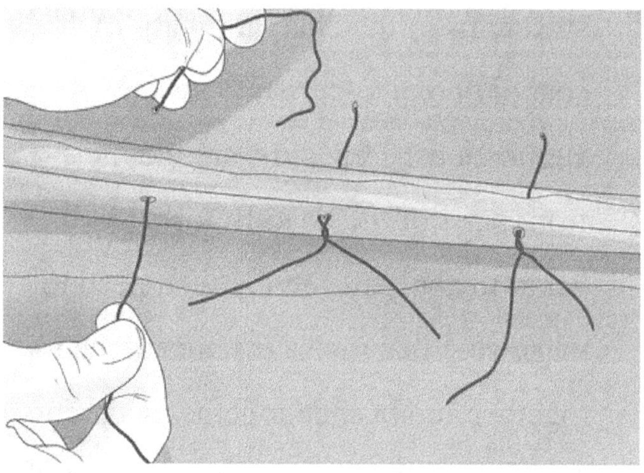

When the epoxy has cured, check to see that all of the joints have been coated with it and that there are no dry patches (areas with no epoxy). If they are, you may begin cutting them and taking out the wire stitches after you have confirmed this.

● Be very careful, since the joints of the panels are still brittle at this phase in the process. Make every effort not to damage the epoxy join, and remove any

and all wires from the boat before you
set sail.

- If you take out a wire and the joint
  opens, you will need to re-epoxy the
  region around the joint and then re-
  install a stitch.

**3-Coat the surface with an epoxy and
wood flour combination/mixture**.

After all of the wire has been removed,
combine equal parts epoxy and wood flour
in a mixing container (really fine sawdust).
Any supplier that specializes in boat
construction should have wood flour. A

fillet is the name given to this particular mixture.

- Combine the wood flour and the epoxy in such a way that the mixture is smooth and creamy; it should not be runny. After applying the epoxy to the joints, apply this fillet to the surface of the epoxy.

- Create a good, smooth bead that is about 1-1/2 to 2 "wide across the middle of each joint, and then apply a fillet in the form of a smooth bead to the inside of the stem end joints.

- Fillet the ends of the stems to a depth of approximately 3/4 "On the inside, it is thick, and although this contributes to the overall weight, it does have the advantage of making the stem nice and sturdy.

- On the other hand, you need to be very cautious not to apply too much epoxy since it has the potential to become brittle.

4-Wrap the inside of the boat with fiberglass tape.

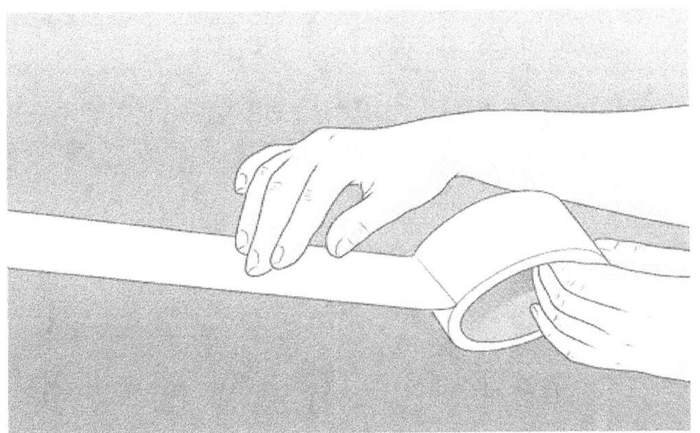

Now it is time to put a 3 to the total "wide fiberglass tape, which is more like a cloth than it is adhesive, to the newly fillet-coated stems and joints.

- Apply yet another layer of epoxy, this time being sure to spread it evenly over the fiberglass until it becomes transparent. To ensure that the junction is as smooth as possible, apply just the amount of epoxy that is necessary to turn the fiberglass transparent, and then remove any excess with a squeegee. Keep in mind that using an excessive amount of epoxy may be just as damaging as applying an insufficient amount.

- When you press down on the fiberglass with the squeegee, be careful not to jar the new fillet mix out of the joint since you don't want to do that. Instead, you should strive to be as mild as you can.

- Once you reach the stems, you should add a 3 "a broad strip of fiberglass was adhered to the inside of the stems (over the fillet). It is important to allow the fiberglass at the stem end to fall down over the central strip of fiberglass tape

since this will make the connection one
that is complete and sturdy.

- After the first layer of epoxy has had
  enough time to harden, you will need to
  apply a second coat of epoxy to these
  tapes. Again, you will need to wait 24
  hours between each application.

5-Sanding the boat.

After the second layer of epoxy has been
applied and allowed to dry, it is time to flip
the boat over. To flip the boat, you'll need
the assistance of another person; just keep
in mind that you need to be extremely

careful, since the boat is still rather fragile at this time.

- Now smooth down the edges of the bottom and lower panel joints using a fine rasp (woodworkers file), taking care not to break the thin plywood as you work. The next step is to use sandpaper with an 80-grit grain to smooth down the edge of the joint, taking care not to sand too deeply into the plywood.

- Sand the whole of the outside of the boat using sandpaper with a grit of 120. Be cautious to wipe up any drips and runs that may have occurred as a result of the epoxy running through the joints. It is important to remember to sand carefully and to avoid sanding into the thin layers of the 1/8' plywood. Doing so will remove material from the

canoe's exterior shell and will create
empty flat patches.

- When you are through sanding, use
cheesecloth to wipe away the excess
dust, and then follow up with
compressed air and a clean cloth to
remove the dust that is more resistant to
being removed. Sweep the floor, then
hold off on moving forward until all of
the dust has been swept up.

**6-Coat the outside of the boat with epoxy
and fiberglass and let it dry.**

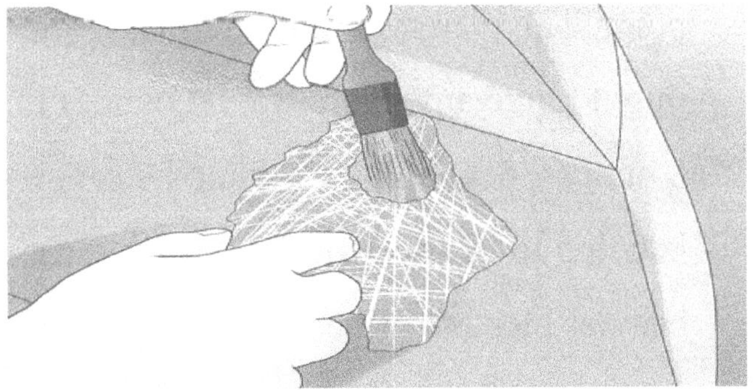

After the dust has dried, you may use a
nice foam brush to apply a layer of epoxy

that is thin and even to the smooth, naked wood that is located on the outside of the canoe. Once again, you will need to wait 24 hours for the epoxy to cure.

- Using paper with a grit of 120, give the epoxy-coated outside of the boat a little sanding. This is not required for any other reason than to give a teeth for the subsequent layer of epoxy and fiberglass to adhere to.

- The outside of the boat has to have fiberglass cloth applied to it at this point. The weight of the fiberglass might range anywhere from 4 ounces to 8 ounces, depending on what the canoe is going to be used for. Because bigger, heavier pieces of fiberglass need more epoxy, the finished canoe will have a greater overall weight as a result.

- Applying a coat of epoxy resin on top of the fiberglass after it has been applied using the same method to the outside of the boat is recommended. If you have never attempted this before, it is highly recommended that you start by learning as much as you can about it via research. If you are well informed, you will be able to perform a much better job on the boat.

7-Shape the fiberglass and epoxy to your liking.

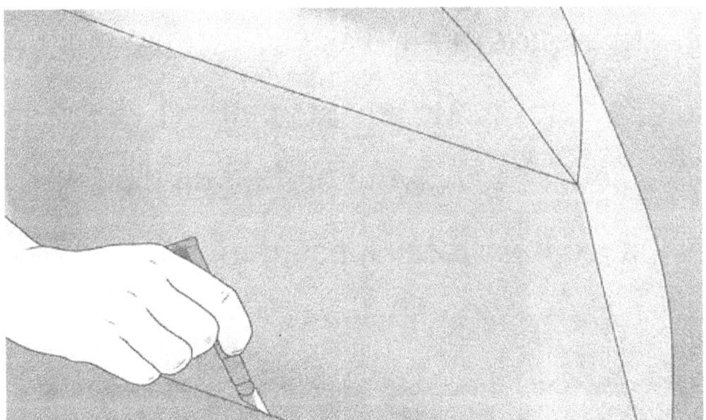

About two hours after applying the epoxy, just before the epoxy begins to set, you will need to cut the fiberglass cloth and epoxy to the desired lengths.

- It will be extremely difficult to cut the extra fiberglass fabric off the edges of the canoe if you wait until the epoxy has had time to solidify before beginning the process.

- Use a razor knife to cut away excess fiberglass fabric around the gunnel's edges. This will allow you to trim the fiberglass cloth. Take care not to cut yourself while you are cutting; you should try to avoid pulling on the fabric since it is still damp and might give you some trouble if it moves.

8-Apply a second layer of epoxy, and then sand the boat thereafter.

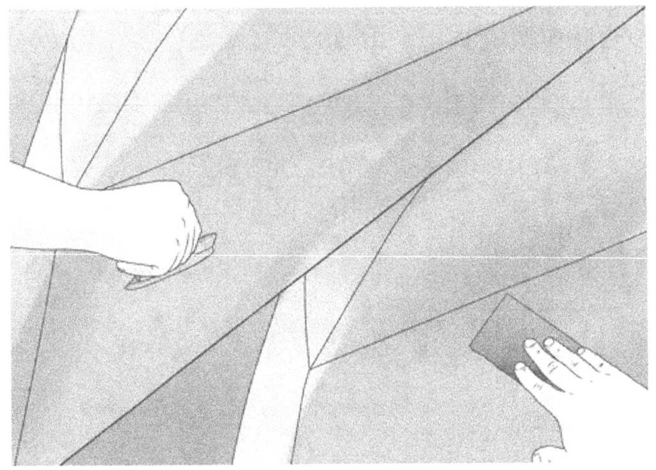

Once the first layer of epoxy that was applied to the fiberglass cloth has been allowed to dry, you will need to apply a second layer in order to fill the weave of the fabric and get a good smooth surface.

- Be aware that depending on the kind and weight of the fabric, it may take more than two coats to completely fill the weave of the fabric.

- After the fiberglass has been adhered and cut, give the outside a quick sanding with sandpaper with a grain of 220, and then remove any and all dust. You may now paint or apply a clear finish to the boat.

Section 3- Putting The Finishing Touches On The Job

1-Turn over the boat completely.

Cautiously turn the boat over so that the right side is facing up, and then secure it in a cradle or slings. It is a good idea to construct a pair of saw horses at this point in order to cradle the canoe and keep it from moving about while you work on the inside of the canoe.

2-Secure the gunnels to the deck.

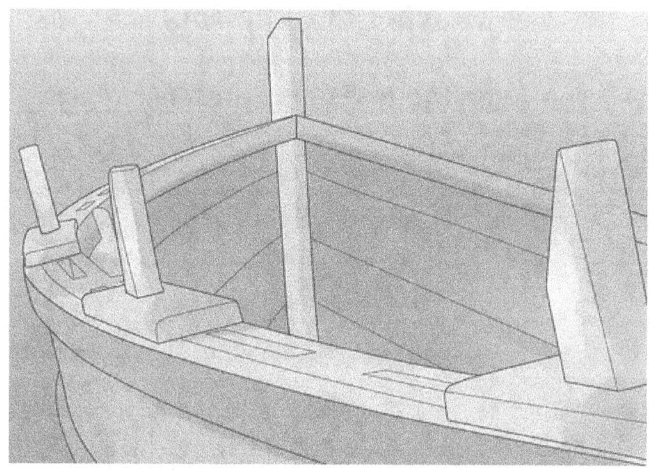

The gunnels of a canoe are the top rails of
the canoe, and they are positioned on the
inner and outside borders/edges of the boat
on both sides.

- The canoe's sides are protected from
  damage by the rub rails, which are also
  known as gunnels, which give the
  canoe its finished appearance.

- Each gunnel need to be about 1-1-1/4
  inches by 3/8-1/2 square, with the top
  outside and inner edges being rounded

over. When attaching the gunnels at the front 24-30, use epoxy in conjunction with brass or bronze screws. Until the time that the epoxy is dry, you may secure the gunnels to the canoe by using both the epoxy and the spring clamps.

- If you take the time and effort to produce a solid fit, you can insert little decks at the stem ends on top of the canoe. These decks may be placed on top of the rails or in the space between the rails. The best-looking decks are flushes.

3-Apply a second layer of varnish or paint that is clear.

It is important to keep in mind that you will have to choose between the two options since epoxy by itself will not survive when it is exposed to the light. After you have completed painting or varnishing the outside of the canoe, it is time to flip it over and either paint or clear coat the inside.

**4-Sand, epoxy, and paint the inside of
the boat before proceeding**.

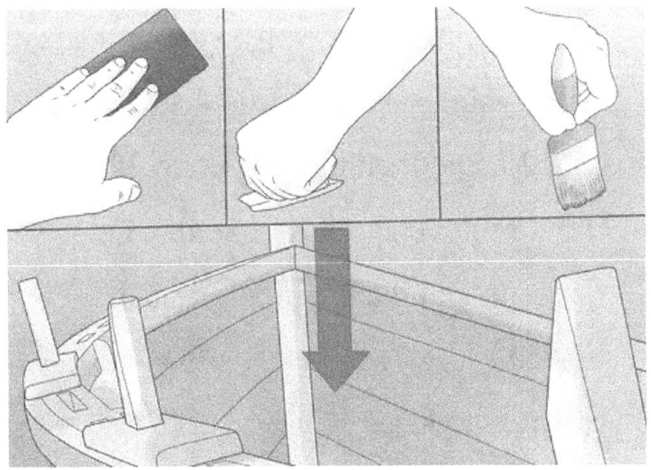

The inside of the boat should be sanded,
and any drips or runs should be removed.
Make every effort not to sand through the
top layer of plywood.

- As soon as all of the sanding is finished,
  it is time to start applying to the interior
  of the boat. This should be done in two
  or three thin layers of epoxy, with a
  wait time of 24 hours in between each
  coat for the best results.

- After you have completed all of these steps, you may create a particularly smooth finish by gently sanding the last layer using sandpaper that has a grain of 120, and then moving up to 220.
- First remove any dust that may be present, and then paint or varnish the inside.

5-Add seatings.

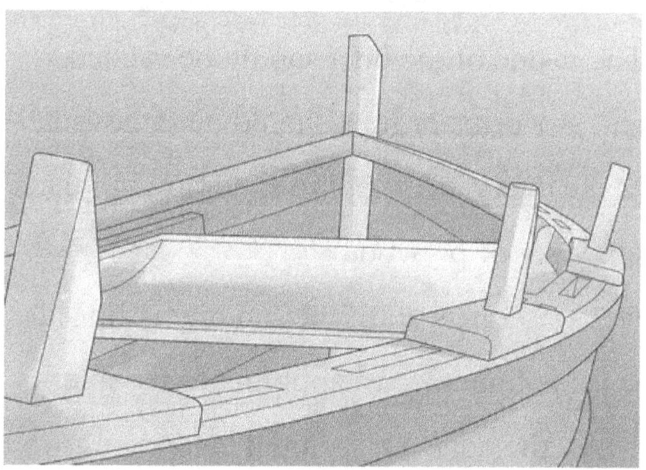

You have the option of installing the seats either before or after you treat the inside of the boat with epoxy.

- Every seat should be around 1-1 1/2 inches deep "rather than dangling from the gunnels of the canoe, from the bottom of the boat.

- It is preferable to maintain the canoe's center of gravity as low in the boat as possible while paddling a light canoe like this one that has a low freeboard.

6-Allow enough time for the boat to dry out.

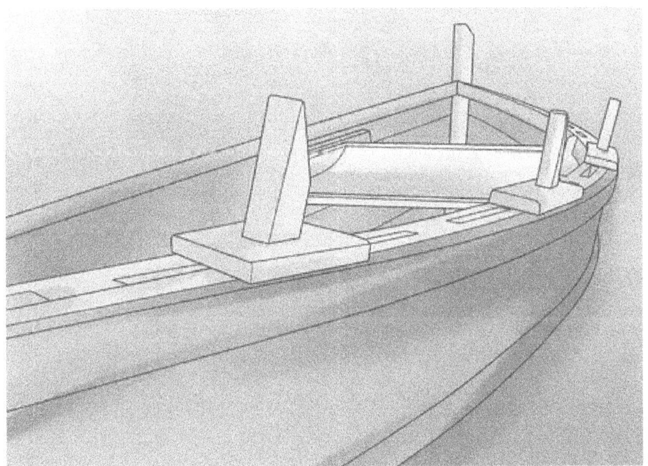

Allow everything to rest for approximately a week; this will allow the individual coats

of epoxy and finish sufficient time to dry
out fully.

CHAPTER TWO

Instructional Guide To Paint a Boat

After many years of your boat being in the water, your boat will start to crack and fade. You are left with two options: you can either take your boat to a professional boat yard to have it repainted or you can do it yourself. It takes a lot of time and work to paint a boat since it starts with prepping the hull and purchasing the paint, but anybody can do it if they have some basic tools and a few free afternoons.

Items You Need

- Marine paint
- Sander
- Solvent
- Primer

- Paintbrush or roller

Part 1-Preparing The Boat

1-Completely clean the boat inside and out.

It is necessary to remove everything from the surface, including the dirt, the sand, the marine life, and the seaweed. In most cases, cleaning the surface of the boat while it is being pulled out of the water is going to be the least difficult option. To get the boat completely clean, you will need a high-pressure hose, a scraper, and some rags.

2-Take all of the boat's hardware and put it away.

You will want to remove as much as you can, right down to any metal window siding that may be there. It's possible that doing this could form a crease between the paint and the hardware, which will then enable water to seep into the fissures and destroy the paint.

- You should use painter's tape to cover anything that you are unable to remove in order to keep it clean and preserve it.

3-Remove the waxy layer off the boat by using a solvent to dissolve the wax.

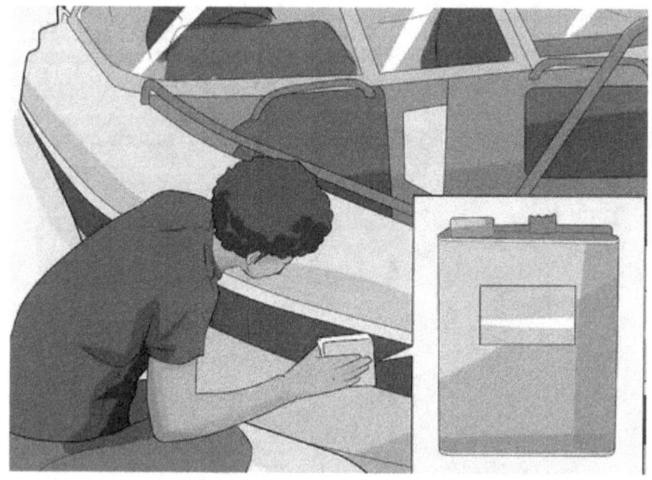

Before you can paint your boat, you will need to remove the oily and waxy finish if you can feel it on the surface. Scrub the waxy finish off with coarse sponges and boat solvents like as Awl-Prep.

- Whether there is still a coating on the surface, you can generally tell if there is one by running your finger over the surface, either the top or the bottom. It has the same sensation as a candle or a vehicle that has just been waxed.

- If you have any uncertainty regarding the coating, you should go over the boat once more. Paint will not adhere to this waxy surface, therefore anything that is there must be removed.

4-Perform any required maintenance or repairs to the surface of the boat.

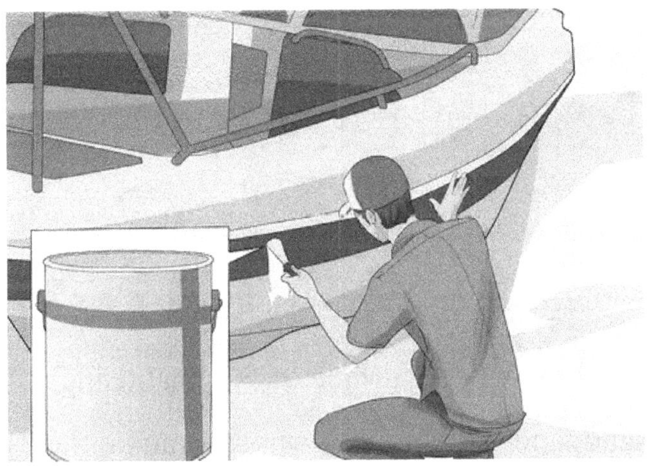

Before beginning the painting process, be sure to fill up any nicks, cracks, or areas of

corrosion to avoid holes or other flaws in
the finished paint job.

● Make sure that any holes that you find
are filled with marine-grade epoxy,
which can be bought at hardware and
boat shops alongside the marine paint.

5-**Sand the boat completely and wholly**.

Sand the whole surface of the boat using
sandpaper with an 80-grit grade and either
a random-orbit sander or a finishing sander.
This provides a surface for the paint to
"grip" to and helps to ensure an equal layer

of paint is applied. If you're not sure what to do, sand off all of the old paint. Sanding requires careful attention to a number of key factors, including the following:

- In the event that the previous layer of paint is peeling or otherwise damaged, you will be required to scrape it and sand it away completely.
- Remove the old paint completely if the new paint that you want to apply is of a different kind than the old paint (for example, vinyl paint against non-vinyl paint).
- Never sand your boat's deck using a belt sander.
- A warning: paint chips may be hazardous to your health, so always be sure to use protective gear while sanding.

Part 2- Painting Of The Boat

1-For the greatest results, paint when the weather is dry and cool.

You do not want the paint work you just had done to be ruined by extreme heat, humidity, or wind. If at all feasible, paint your boat on a day with temperatures ranging from from 50 to 80 degrees Fahrenheit and a relative humidity level of approximately 60 percent.

- If you have access to a covered space, paint your boat there whenever you can.

**2-Make sure that you paint your boat
with the appropriate color**.

There is a wide variety of paint available
on the market for use on boats, ranging
from gel coatings and simple enamels to
intricate paint mixtures that need two steps
to complete. If you are going to paint your
own boat, the one-step polyurethane paint
is surely going to provide you the greatest
"bang for your money."

- Two step Polyurethane paint requires more accurate mixing and application procedures, but it lasts far longer.
- The majority of gel coatings, with the exception of more costly, high-end alternatives, will yellow within one to two years.

3-Apply one to two complete layers of primer.

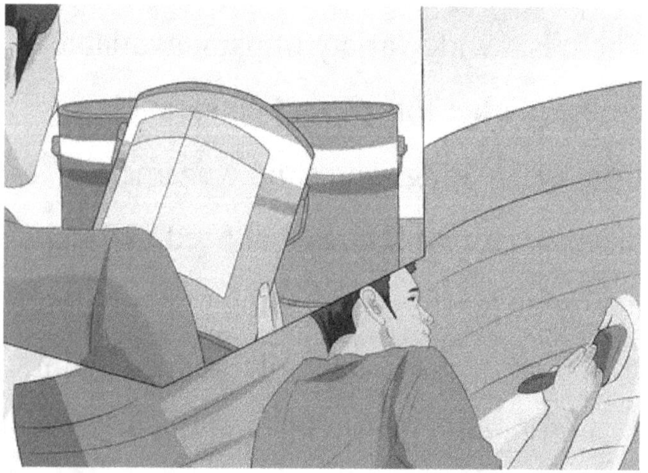

By examining the labels on the primer and paint cans, you can determine whether or not they are compatible with one another.

The use of primer strengthens the
connection between the paint and the boat
and prevents breaking and bubbling.

● After the first layer has had time to dry,
give the boat a gentle sanding using
sandpaper that has a grit of 300, and
then apply a second coat.

**4-Complete the painting of the boat by
using a roller and a brush.**

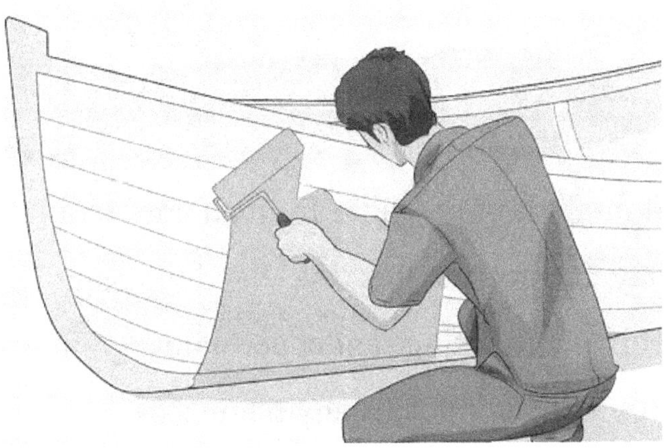

It is important to work swiftly, beginning
the painting process from the stern of the
boat and working your way up. Paint

rollers are ideal for covering large areas
quickly, whereas brushes are better suited
for working on more detailed areas.

**5-Once the paint has completely dry,
give it a little sanding**.

It might take anything from an hour to a
day to complete this task. Sand the paint
very gently using sandpaper with a grain of
300. This eliminates any blemishes,
problems, or bubbles in the paint.

6-Add an additional two to three coats of paint.

After each layer of paint has dried, give the boat a little sanding. Even if it takes time, putting two or three coats of paint that are completely clean assures that your boat will not deteriorate or break in the years to come.

CHAPTER THREE

Instructional Guide To Fiberglass Boat

There are several advantages to using fiberglass for the construction of boats. The ease with which it may be repaired is second only to its remarkable longevity/durability among these advantages. You can repair holes in boats in as little as an afternoon, and you can fiberglass a boat in little more than a few days. The use of epoxy resin in the process of fiberglassing a boat is covered in this chapter.

Items You Need

- Dewaxing solvent
- Mold release
- Belt sander

- Fiberglass cloth

- Protective agent

- Fiberglass resin and hardener

Steps

1-Get the boat ready for the process of fiberglassing. You will first need to prepare your boat before beginning the process of putting fiberglass to it, so keep that in mind. It is necessary to give some consideration to a variety of various forms of preparations.

- Removing any unnecessary objects from the boat's holdings at the bottom. You will need to remove the keel, any lift pegs or rails, and anything else that should not be coated with fiberglass before you can proceed with the fiberglassing process.

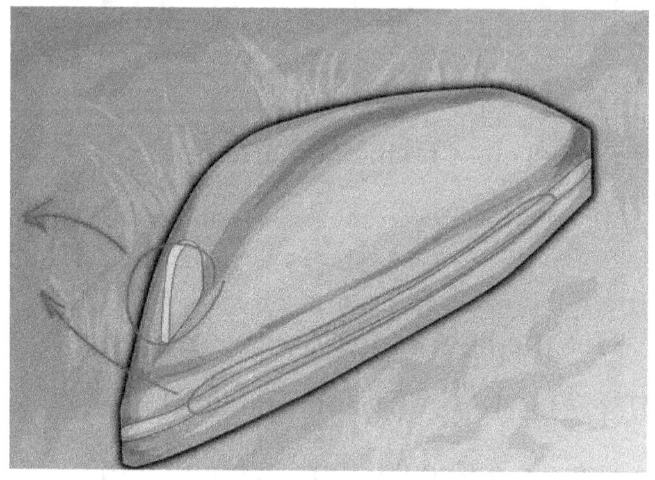

- Use the right filler to patch/repair any holes that you find. In order to repair a hole, first cut out the damaged part, then wash the area and apply a dewaxing solvent, then grind the area with a disk sander, then apply a laminate or acrylic patch to the outside of the hull with polyvinyl alcohol (PVA) mold release, and finally apply a fiberglass patch that has been measured and cut to fit the hole. Apply resin, then if required, repeat the procedure of

applying fiberglass and resin, and finish
by adding hardener.

- Take sufficient time to clean the inside
  of the boat's hull thoroughly. It is
  important to remove any debris,
  barnacles, dust, grime, and mold that
  may be on the hull.

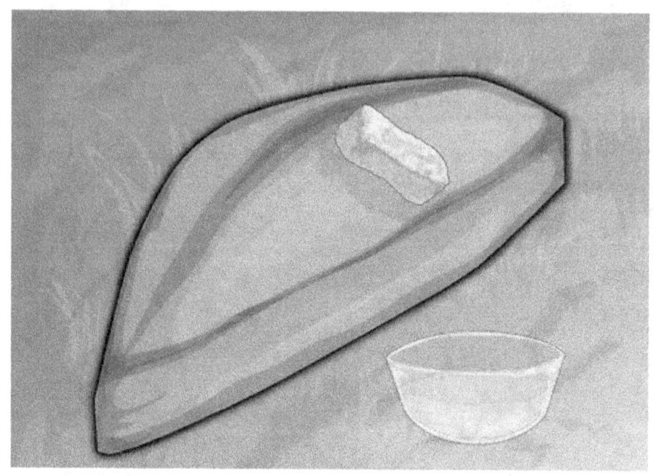

- The boat should be sanded.
  Roughening up the surface just a little
  bit will provide the greatest effects.
  Rippling may appear if an excessive
  amount of sanding is done.

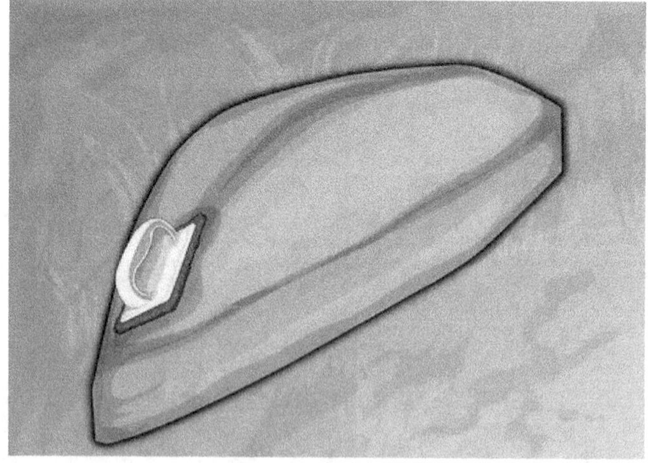

2-After properly mixing the resin and the hardener in accordance with the instructions on the box, immediately pour the resulting solution into a paint tray.

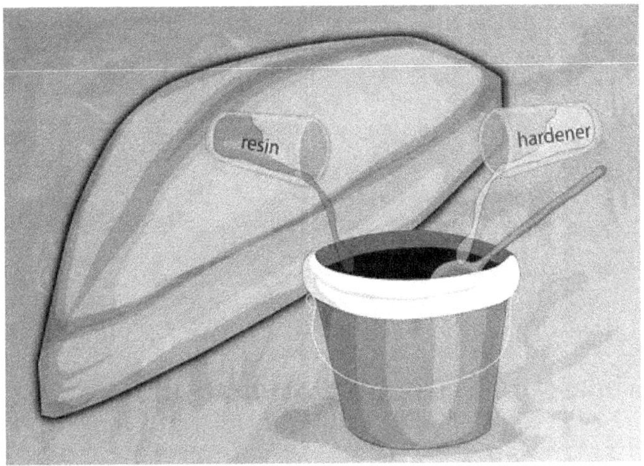

After around thirty minutes, the solution ought to have greatly hardened and be ready to be applied to the hull of the boat in preparation for the next step.

3-Add the first coat of resin to the surface.

This first coat is referred to as the *seal coat*. Make sure to use firm pressure and directed strokes while working with a foam roller to ensure that the resin is distributed as evenly as possible. Before continuing your work on the hull, you should hold off until the surface has lost its sticky quality

**4-Get the fiberglass cloth ready, and
then install it**.

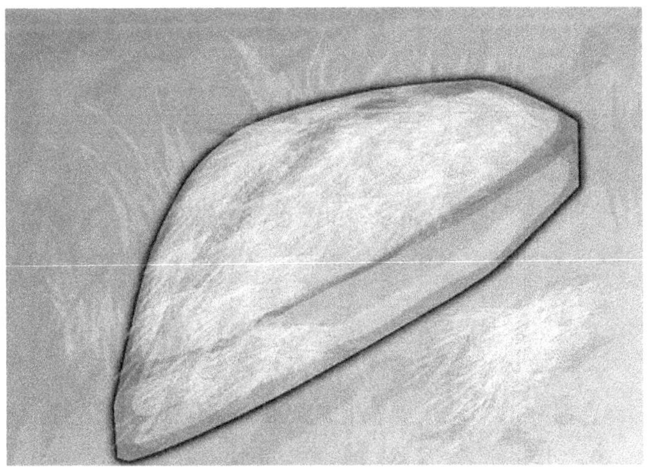

To create the desired shape, cut the
fiberglass cloth. Tape, tacks, or staples may
be used to attach the fiberglass cloth to the
hull of the boat.

5-**Add a second coat of resin to the surface.**

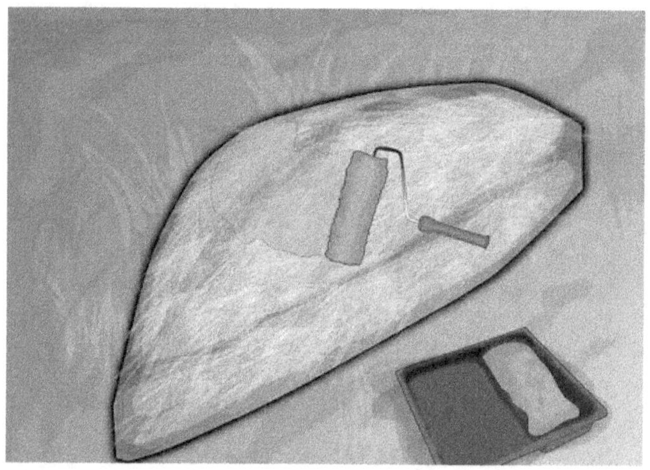

The name given to this coat is the *bond coat*. Think about sanding the hull once again if some time has passed since the last time you did it. Applying the bond coat over the fiberglass cloth should be done starting at one end of the hull and working your way to the other. Before the bond coat has had a chance to fully harden, it is necessary for you to remove the substance

that was used to connect the fiberglass
fabric to the boat.

**6-Add another coat of resin to the
surface.**

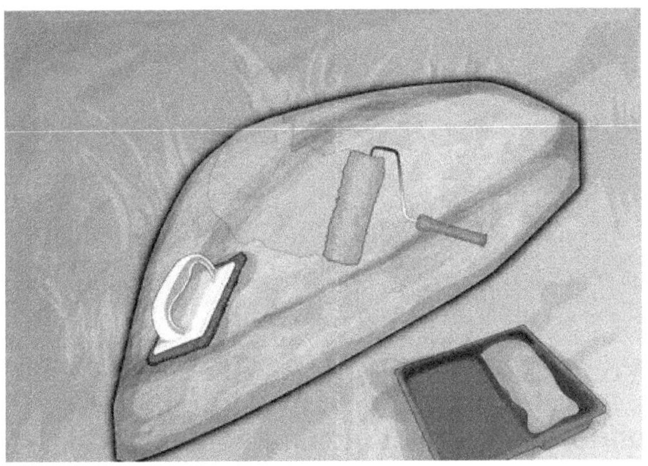

The name "*fill coat*" refers to this particular
coat. Wait for the previous application to
dry completely before applying the next
one. If a considerable amount of time has
passed since you last cleaned and sanded
the hull, you should do it once again.

7-Add one last layer of resin to the surface.

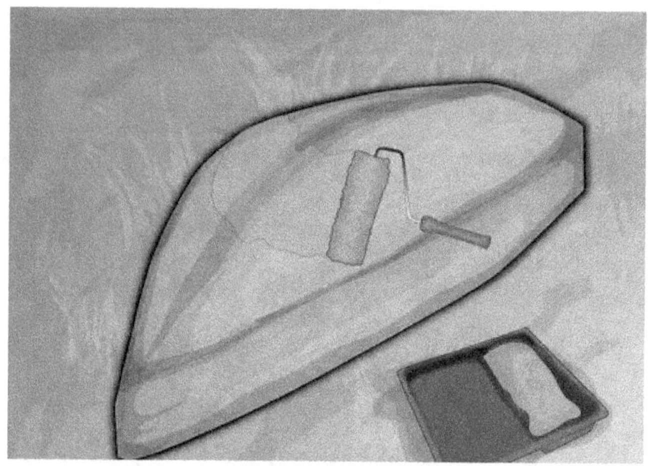

You should be able to sand the hull uniformly without breaking the fabric if the finish coat is thick enough. The finish coat should be smooth and even, and it should also be thick enough.

8-At this time, you should sand the hull.

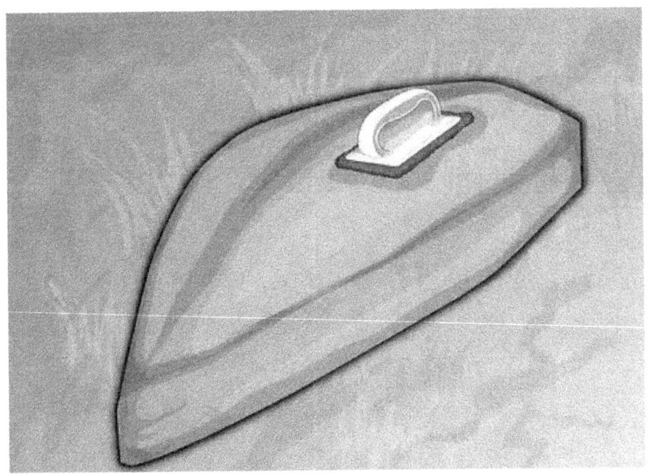

Allow the final coat to dry for a sufficient amount of time, ideally overnight. Start with a finer grit paper and work your way up to a coarser one as you go.

9-Add some kind of protective agent.

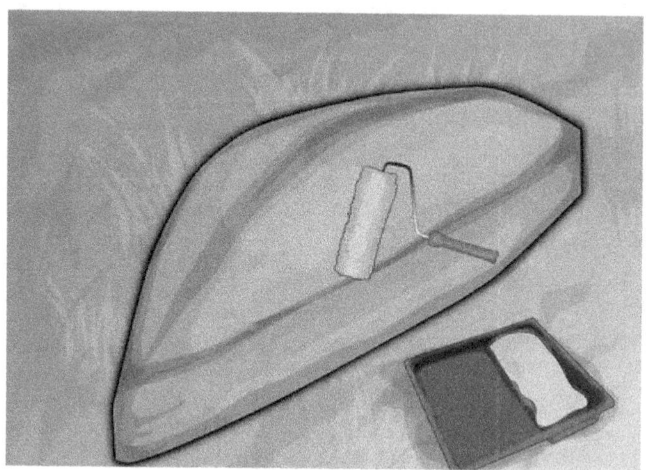

This might be paint or another kind of finish for the boat hull. To use the protective agent properly, follow the instructions on the packaging.